THE COMMON CORE

Clarifying Expectations for Teachers & Students

ENGLISH LANGUAGE ARTS

Grades 9 – 10

Created and Presented by
Align, Assess, Achieve

Mc Graw Hill Education

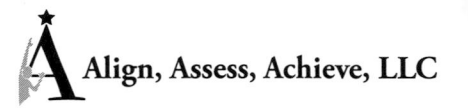
Align, Assess, Achieve, LLC

Align, Assess, Achieve; *The Common Core: Clarifying Expectations for Teachers &*
Students. Grades 9-10

STEM McGraw-Hill is committed to providing instructional materials in Science,
Technology, Engineering, and Mathematics (STEM) that give all students a solid
foundation, one that prepares them for college and careers in the 21st century.

Send all inquiries to:
McGraw-Hill Education
STEM Learning Solutions Center
8787 Orion Place
Columbus, OH 43240

ISBN: 978-007-662962-6
MHID: 0-07-662962-7

Printed in the United States of America.

2 3 4 5 6 7 8 9 GLO 17 16 15 14 13 12

STEM

Our mission is to provide educational resources
that enable students to become the problem solvers
of the 21st century and inspire them to explore
careers within Science, Technology, Engineering,
and Mathematics (STEM) related fields.

Acknowledgements

This book integrates the Common Core State Standards – a framework for educating students to be competitive at an international level – with well-researched instructional planning strategies for achieving the goals of the CCSS. Our work is rooted in the thinking of brilliant educators, such as Grant Wiggins, Jay McTighe, and Rick Stiggins, and enriched by our work with a great number of inspiring teachers, administrators, and parents. We hope this book provides a meaningful contribution to the ongoing conversation around educating lifelong, passionate learners.

We would like to thank many talented contributors who helped create *The Common Core: Clarifying Expectations for Teachers and Students.* Our authors, Lani Meyers and Mindy Holmes, for their intelligence, persistence, and love of teaching; Graphic Designer Thomas Davis, for his creative talents and good nature through many trials; Editors, Laura Gage and Dr. Teresa Dempsey, for their educational insights and encouragement; Director of book editing and production Josh Steskal, for his feedback, organization, and unwavering patience; Our spouses, Andrew Bainbridge and Tawnya Holman, who believe in our mission and have, through their unconditional support and love, encouraged us to take risks and grow.

Katy Bainbridge
Bob Holman
Co-Founders
Align, Assess, Achieve, LLC

Executive Editors: *Katy Bainbridge and Bob Holman*
Authors: *Mindy Holmes and Lani Meyers*
Contributing Authors: *Teresa Dempsey, Katy Bainbridge and Bob Holman*
Graphic Design & Layout: *Thomas Davis; thomasanceldesign.com*
Director of Book Editing & Production: *Josh Steskal*

Introduction

Purpose

The Common Core State Standards (CCSS) provide educators across the nation with a shared vision for student achievement. They also provide a shared challenge: how to interpret the standards and use them in a meaningful way? Clarifying the Common Core was designed to facilitate the transition to the CCSS at the district, building, and classroom level.

Organization

Clarifying the Common Core presents content from two sources: the CCSS and Align, Assess, Achieve. Content from the CCSS is located in the top section of each page and includes the strand, CCR, and grade level standard. The second section of each page contains content created by Align, Assess, Achieve – Enduring Understandings, Essential Questions, Suggested Learning Targets, and Vocabulary. The black bar at the bottom of the page contains the CCSS standard identifier. A sample page can be found in the next section.

Planning for Instruction and Assessment

This book was created to foster meaningful instruction of the CCSS. This requires planning both quality instruction and assessment. Designing and using quality assessments is key to high-quality instruction (Stiggins et al.). Assessment should accurately measure the intended learning and should inform further instruction. This is only possible when teachers and students have a clear vision of the intended learning. When planning instruction it helps to ask two questions, "Where am I taking my students?" and "How will we get there?" The first question refers to the big picture and is addressed with **Enduring Understandings** and **Essential Questions**. The second question points to the instructional process and is addressed by **Learning Targets**.

Where Am I Taking My Students?

When planning, it is useful to think about the larger, lasting instructional concepts as **Enduring Understandings**. Enduring Understandings are rooted in multiple units of instruction throughout the year and are often utilized K-12. These concepts represent the lasting understandings that transcend your content. Enduring Understandings serve as the ultimate goal of a teacher's instructional planning. Although tempting to share with students initially, we do not recommend telling students the Enduring Understanding in advance. Rather, Enduring Understandings are developed through meaningful engagement with an Essential Question.

(continued on next page)

Essential Questions work in concert with Enduring Understandings to ignite student curiosity. These questions help students delve deeper and make connections between the concepts and the content they are learning. Essential Questions are designed with the student in mind and do not have an easy answer; rather, they are used to spark inquiry into the deeper meanings (Wiggins and McTighe). Therefore, we advocate frequent use of Essential Questions with students. It is sometimes helpful to think of the Enduring Understanding as the answer to the Essential Question.

How Will We Get There?

If Enduring Understandings and Essential Questions represent the larger, conceptual ideas, then what guides the learning of specific knowledge, reasoning, and skills? These are achieved by using **Learning Targets**. Learning Targets represent a logical, student friendly progression of teaching and learning. Targets are the scaffolding students climb as they progress towards deeper meaning.

There are four types of learning targets, based on what students are asked to do: knowledge, reasoning/understanding, skill, and product (Stiggins et al.). When selecting Learning Targets, teachers need to ask, "What is the goal of instruction?" After answering this question, select the target or targets that align to the instructional goal.

Instructional Goal	Target Type	Key Verbs
Recall basic information and facts	Knowledge (K)	Name, identify, describe
Think and develop an understanding	Reasoning/ Understanding (R)	Explain, compare and contrast, predict
Apply knowledge and reasoning	Skill (S)	Use, solve, calculate
Synthesize to create original work	Product (P)	Create, write, present

Adapted from Stiggins et al. *Classroom Assessment for Student Learning*. (Portland: ETS, 2006). Print.

Keep in mind that the Enduring Understandings, Essential Questions, and Learning Targets in this book are suggestions. Modify and combine the content as necessary to meet your instructional needs. Quality instruction consists of clear expectations, ongoing assessment, and effective feedback. Taken together, these promote meaningful instruction that facilitates student mastery of the Common Core State Standards.

References

Stiggins, Rick, Jan Chappuis, Judy Arter, and Steve Chappuis. *Classroom Assessment for Student Learning*. 2nd. Portland, OR: ETS, 2006.

Wiggins, Grant, and Jay McTighe. *Understanding by Design, Expanded 2nd Edition*. 2nd. Alexandria, VA: ASCD, 2005.

Page Organization

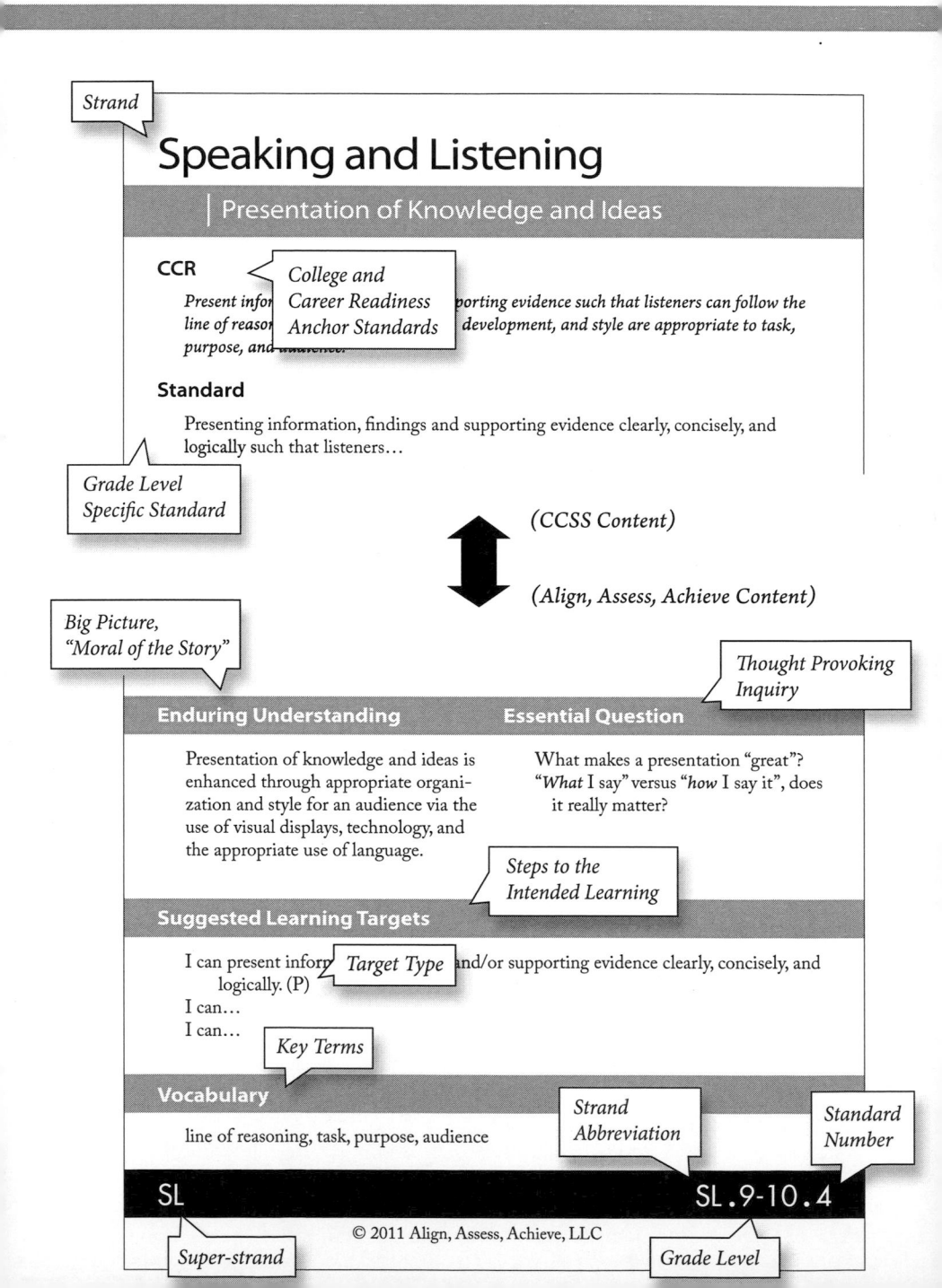

Strand

Speaking and Listening

Presentation of Knowledge and Ideas

CCR

College and Career Readiness Anchor Standards

Present infor... ...porting evidence such that listeners can follow the line of reaso... ...development, and style are appropriate to task, purpose, and ...

Standard

Presenting information, findings and supporting evidence clearly, concisely, and logically such that listeners...

Grade Level Specific Standard

(CCSS Content)

(Align, Assess, Achieve Content)

Big Picture, "Moral of the Story"

Thought Provoking Inquiry

Enduring Understanding

Presentation of knowledge and ideas is enhanced through appropriate organization and style for an audience via the use of visual displays, technology, and the appropriate use of language.

Essential Question

What makes a presentation "great"? "*What* I say" versus "*how* I say it", does it really matter?

Steps to the Intended Learning

Suggested Learning Targets

I can present infor... *Target Type* ...and/or supporting evidence clearly, concisely, and logically. (P)

I can...

I can...

Key Terms

Vocabulary

line of reasoning, task, purpose, audience

Strand Abbreviation

Standard Number

SL

SL.9-10.4

Super-strand

Grade Level

© 2011 Align, Assess, Achieve, LLC

Literature

CCR

Read closely to determine what the text says explicitly and to make logical inferences from it; cite specific textual evidence when writing or speaking to support conclusions drawn from the text.

Standard

Cite strong and thorough textual evidence to support analysis of what the text says explicitly as well as inferences drawn from the text.

Enduring Understanding

Effective readers use a variety of strategies to make sense of key ideas and details presented in text.

Essential Questions

What do good readers do?
Am I clear about what I just read?
How do I know?

Suggested Learning Targets

I can define textual evidence (a "word for word" support format). (K)
I can define inference and explain how a reader uses textual evidence to reach a logical conclusion ("based on what I've read, it's most likely true that…"). (R)
I can read closely and find answers explicitly in text (right there answers) and answers that require an inference. (S)
I can analyze an author's words and determine multiple pieces of textual evidence that strongly and thoroughly support both explicit and inferential questions. (R)

Vocabulary

textual evidence, analyze, inference, explicit

R   RL.9-10.1

Literature

CCR

Determine central ideas or themes of a text and analyze their development; summarize the key supporting details and ideas.

Standard

Determine a theme or central idea of a text and analyze in detail its development over the course of the text, including how it emerges and is shaped and refined by specific details; provide an objective summary of the text.

Enduring Understanding

Effective readers use a variety of strategies to make sense of key ideas and details presented in text.

Essential Questions

What do good readers do?
Am I clear about what I just read?
How do I know?

Suggested Learning Targets

I can define theme (a central idea or lesson the author is revealing – *Honesty is the best policy.*). (K)
I can analyze plot (the events that happen) to determine a theme (author's overall message). (R)
I can determine how specific details in the text reveal and continually refine a theme. (R)
I can define summary (a shortened version of the text that states key points). (K)
I can compose an objective summary stating the key points of the text without adding my own opinions or feelings. (P)

Vocabulary

theme, central idea, summary, objective

R
RL.9-10.2

Literature

CCR

Analyze how and why individuals, events, and ideas develop and interact over the course of a text.

Standard

Analyze how complex characters (e.g., those with multiple or conflicting motivations) develop over the course of a text, interact with other characters, and advance the plot or develop the theme.

Enduring Understanding

Effective readers use a variety of strategies to make sense of key ideas and details presented in text.

Essential Questions

What do good readers do?
Am I clear about what I just read?
How do I know?

Suggested Learning Targets

I can identify and explain the role of complex characters in a text. (R)
I can analyze how complex characters develop over the course of a text. (R)
I can analyze how characters develop through their interactions with others. (R)
I can analyze how complex characters advance the plot of a text and/or contribute to the development the theme. (R)

Vocabulary

complex character, theme

R   RL.9-10.3

Literature

CCR

Interpret words and phrases as they are used in a text, including determining technical, connotative, and figurative meanings, and analyze how specific word choices shape meaning or tone.

Standard

Determine the meaning of words and phrases as they are used in the text, including figurative and connotative meanings; analyze the cumulative impact of specific word choices on meaning and tone (e.g., how the language evokes a sense of time and place; how it sets a formal or informal tone).

Enduring Understanding

Analyzing texts for structure, purpose, and viewpoint allows an effective reader to gain insight and strengthen understanding.

Essential Questions

Author's choice: Why does it matter? What makes a story a "great" story?

Suggested Learning Targets

I can define and identify various forms of figurative language (e.g., simile, metaphor, hyperbole, personification, alliteration, assonance, onomatopoeia). (K)

I can distinguish between literal language (it means exactly what it says) and figurative language (sometimes what you say is not exactly what you mean). (K)

I can recognize the difference between denotative meanings (all words have a dictionary definition) and connotative meanings (some words carry feeling). (K)

I can analyze why authors choose specific words to evoke a particular meaning or tone. (R)

I can analyze how specific word choices build upon one another to create a cumulative (collective) impact on the overall meaning and tone of a text. (R)

Vocabulary

figurative language, literal language, denotative meaning, connotative meaning, cumulative

R   RL.9-10.4

Literature

CCR

Analyze the structure of texts, including how specific sentences, paragraphs, and larger portions of the text (e.g., a section, chapter, scene, or stanza) relate to each other and the whole.

Standard

Analyze how an author's choices concerning how to structure a text, order events within it (e.g., parallel plots), and manipulate time (e.g., pacing, flashbacks) create such effects as mystery, tension, or surprise.

Enduring Understanding

Analyzing texts for structure, purpose, and viewpoint allows an effective reader to gain insight and strengthen understanding.

Essential Questions

Author's choice: Why does it matter? What makes a story a "great" story?

Suggested Learning Targets

I can identify different literary text structures (e.g., narrative, poem, drama). (K)
I can analyze a text and determine why an author chose to present his/her text using a particular structure. (R)
I can analyze a text and determine why an author organized events in a particular order (e.g., parallel plot – Two main characters have separate but related story lines that merge in the end.). (R)
I can analyze a text and determine how an author manipulates time (e.g., flashback – When a character recalls an experience that occurred in the past.). (R)
I can analyze how an author's choice of text structure creates such effects as mystery, tension, or surprise. (R)

Vocabulary

text structure

R   RL.9-10.5

Literature

CCR

Assess how point of view or purpose shapes the content and style of a text.

Standard

Analyze a particular point of view or cultural experience reflected in a work of literature from outside the United States, drawing on a wide reading of world literature.

Enduring Understanding

Analyzing texts for structure, purpose, and viewpoint allows an effective reader to gain insight and strengthen understanding.

Essential Questions

Author's choice: Why does it matter? What makes a story a "great" story?

Suggested Learning Targets

I can explain how the point of view or cultural experience (e.g., government, role of women) found in various works of world literature differs from works of literature written in the United States. (R)
I can analyze multiple texts of world literature to gain insight into the point of view of other societies and cultures. (R)

Vocabulary

point of view, cultural experience, world literature

R   RL.9-10.6

Literature

CCR

*Integrate and evaluate content presented in diverse media and formats, including visually and quantitatively, as well as in words.**

Standard

Analyze the representation of a subject or a key scene in two different artistic mediums, including what is emphasized or absent in each treatment (e.g., Auden's "Musée des Beaux Arts" and Breughel's *Landscape with the Fall of Icarus*).

*Please see "Research to Build Knowledge" in Writing and "Comprehension and Collaboration" in Speaking and Listening for additional standards relevant to gathering, assessing, and applying information from print and digital sources.

Enduring Understanding	Essential Questions
To gain keener insight into the integration of knowledge and ideas, effective readers analyze and evaluate content, reasoning, and claims in diverse formats.	In what ways does creative choice impact an audience? Whose story is it, and why does it matter?

Suggested Learning Targets

I can identify a subject or a key scene that is portrayed in two different artistic mediums (e.g., poetry, painting, drama). (K)

I can determine what is emphasized or absent in each artistic medium. (R)

I can analyze the impact of a particular subject or key scene from another artistic medium. (R)

Vocabulary

artistic medium

R   RL.9-10.7

Literature

CCR

Delineate and evaluate the argument and specific claims in a text, including the validity of the reasoning as well as the relevance and sufficiency of the evidence.

Standard

(Not applicable to literature)

(No Common Core State Standard #8 for Reading and Literature)

Literature

CCR

Analyze how two or more texts address similar themes or topics in order to build knowledge or to compare the approaches the authors take.

Standard

Analyze how an author draws on and transforms source material in a specific work (e.g., how Shakespeare treats a theme or topic from Ovid or the Bible or how a later author draws on a play by Shakespeare).

Enduring Understanding

To gain keener insight into the integration of knowledge and ideas, effective readers analyze and evaluate content, reasoning, and claims in diverse formats.

Essential Questions

In what ways does creative choice impact an audience?

Whose story is it, and why does it matter?

Suggested Learning Targets

I can identify source material from one author found in the work of another. (K)

I can analyze how authors interpret and transform themes, events, topics, etc. from source material. (R)

I can critique various works that have drawn on or transformed the same source material and explain the varied interpretations of different authors. (S)

Vocabulary

source material, critique

R

RL.9-10.9

Literature

CCR

Read and comprehend complex literary and informational texts independently and proficiently.

Standard

By the end of grade 9, read and comprehend literature, including stories, dramas, and poems, in the grades 9–10 text complexity band proficiently, with scaffolding as needed at the high end of the range.

Enduring Understanding

Students who are college and career ready read and interpret a variety of complex texts with confidence and independence.

Essential Questions

What do good readers do?
Am I clear about what I just read?
How do I know?

Suggested Learning Targets

I can closely read complex grade level texts. (S)
I can reread a text to find more information or clarify ideas. (S)
I can use reading strategies (e.g., ask questions, make connections, take notes, make inferences, visualize, re-read) to help me understand difficult complex text. (S)

Vocabulary

reading strategy, comprehension

R   RL.9.10

Literature

CCR

Read and comprehend complex literary and informational texts independently and proficiently.

Standard

By the end of grade 10, read and comprehend literature, including stories, dramas, and poems, at the high end of the grades 9–10 text complexity band independently and proficiently.

Enduring Understanding

Students who are college and career ready read and interpret a variety of complex texts with confidence and independence.

Essential Questions

What do good readers do?
Am I clear about what I just read?
How do I know?

Suggested Learning Targets

I can closely read complex grade level texts. (S)
I can reread a text to find more information or clarify ideas. (S)
I can use reading strategies (e.g., ask questions, make connections, take notes, make inferences, visualize, re-read) to help me understand difficult complex text. (S)

Vocabulary

reading strategy, comprehension

R   RL.10.10

Informational Text

CCR

Read closely to determine what the text says explicitly and to make logical inferences from it; cite specific textual evidence when writing or speaking to support conclusions drawn from the text.

Standard

Cite strong and thorough textual evidence to support analysis of what the text says explicitly as well as inferences drawn from the text.

Enduring Understanding

Effective readers use a variety of strategies to make sense of key ideas and details presented in text.

Essential Questions

What do good readers do?
Am I clear about what I just read?
How do I know?

Suggested Learning Targets

I can define textual evidence (a "word for word" support format). (K)
I can define inference and explain how a reader uses textual evidence to reach a logical conclusion ("based on what I've read, it's most likely true that…"). (R)
I can read closely and find answers explicitly in text (right there answers) and answers that require an inference. (S)
I can analyze an author's words and determine multiple pieces of textual evidence that strongly and thoroughly support both explicit and inferential questions. (R)

Vocabulary

textual evidence, inference, explicit

R   RI.9-10.1

Informational Text

CCR

Determine central ideas or themes of a text and analyze their development; summarize the key supporting details and ideas.

Standard

Determine a central idea of a text and analyze its development over the course of the text, including how it emerges and is shaped and refined by specific details; provide an objective summary of the text.

Enduring Understanding

Effective readers use a variety of strategies to make sense of key ideas and details presented in text.

Essential Questions

What do good readers do?
Am I clear about what I just read?
How do I know?

Suggested Learning Targets

I can define central idea (main point in a piece of writing). (K)
I can analyze how specific details developed over the course of a text shape and refine a central idea. (R)
I can compose an objective summary stating the key points of the text without adding my own opinions or feelings. (P)

Vocabulary

central idea, objective

R   RI.9-10.2

Informational Text

CCR

Analyze how and why individuals, events, and ideas develop and interact over the course of a text.

Standard

Analyze how the author unfolds an analysis or series of ideas or events, including the order in which the points are made, how they are introduced and developed, and the connections that are drawn between them.

Enduring Understanding

Effective readers use a variety of strategies to make sense of key ideas and details presented in text.

Essential Questions

What do good readers do?
Am I clear about what I just read?
How do I know?

Suggested Learning Targets

I can determine the overall analysis, ideas, or events being conveyed by an author. (R)
I can analyze how a text unfolds and determine the impact that the order, development, and/or connections between points have on the reader. (R)

Vocabulary

analysis

R   RI.9-10.3

Informational Text

CCR

Interpret words and phrases as they are used in a text, including determining technical, connotative, and figurative meanings, and analyze how specific word choices shape meaning or tone.

Standard

Determine the meaning of words and phrases as they are used in a text, including figurative, connotative, and technical meanings; analyze the cumulative impact of specific word choices on meaning and tone (e.g., how the language of a court opinion differs from that of a newspaper).

Enduring Understanding

Analyzing texts for structure, purpose, and viewpoint allows an effective reader to gain insight and strengthen understanding.

Essential Questions

Author's choice: Why does it matter? What makes a story a "great" story?

Suggested Learning Targets

I can define and identify various forms of figurative language (e.g., simile, metaphor, hyperbole, personification, alliteration, onomatopoeia). (K)

I can distinguish between literal language (it means exactly what it says) and figurative language (sometimes what you say is not exactly what you mean). (K)

I can recognize the difference between denotative meanings (all words have a dictionary definition) and connotative meanings (some words carry feeling). (K)

I can recognize words that have technical meaning and understand their purpose in a specific text (e.g., "stem" in an article about flowers versus "stem" in an article about cell research). (R)

I can analyze how specific word choices build on one another to create a cumulative impact on the overall meaning and tone of a text. (R)

Vocabulary

figurative language, literal language, denotative meaning, connotative meaning, technical meaning, tone, mood, cumulative

R   RI.9-10.4

Informational Text

CCR

Analyze the structure of texts, including how specific sentences, paragraphs, and larger portions of the text (e.g., a section, chapter, scene, or stanza) relate to each other and the whole.

Standard

Analyze in detail how an author's ideas or claims are developed and refined by particular sentences, paragraphs, or larger portions of a text (e.g., a section or chapter).

Enduring Understanding

Analyzing texts for structure, purpose, and viewpoint allows an effective reader to gain insight and strengthen understanding.

Essential Questions

Author's choice: Why does it matter?
What makes a story a "great" story?

Suggested Learning Targets

I can identify particular sentences, paragraphs, or larger portions of a text that support an author's ideas or claims. (R)
I can analyze and explain how the role of particular sentences, paragraphs, or larger portions of a text helps to develop and refine the author's ideas or claims. (R)

Vocabulary

claim, refine

R   RI.9-10.5

Informational Text

CCR

Assess how point of view or purpose shapes the content and style of a text.

Standard

Determine an author's point of view or purpose in a text and analyze how an author uses rhetoric to advance that point of view or purpose.

Enduring Understanding

Analyzing texts for structure, purpose, and viewpoint allows an effective reader to gain insight and strengthen understanding.

Essential Questions

Author's choice: Why does it matter? What makes a story a "great" story?

Suggested Learning Targets

I can define point of view as how the author feels about the situation/topic of a text. (K)

I can determine an author's point of view (*What do I know about the author's opinions, values, and/or beliefs?*) and explain his/her purpose for writing the text. (R)

I can define rhetoric (a technique an author uses to persuade a reader to consider a topic from a different perspective). (K)

I can identify when an author uses rhetoric and analyze how the rhetoric strengthens his/her point of view or purpose. (R)

Vocabulary

point of view, purpose, rhetoric

R

RI.9-10.6

Informational Text

CCR

Integrate and evaluate content presented in diverse media and formats, including visually and quantitatively, as well as in words.*

Standard

Analyze various accounts of a subject told in different mediums (e.g., a person's life story in both print and multimedia), determining which details are emphasized in each account.

*Please see "Research to Build Knowledge" in Writing and "Comprehension and Collaboration" in Speaking and Listening for additional standards relevant to gathering, assessing, and applying information from print and digital sources.

Enduring Understanding

To gain keener insight into the integration of knowledge and ideas, effective readers analyze and evaluate content, reasoning, and claims in diverse formats.

Essential Questions

In what ways does creative choice impact an audience?
Whose story is it, and why does it matter?

Suggested Learning Targets

I can identify various accounts of the same subject that are presented in different mediums (e.g., audio, video, multimedia). (K)
I can analyze various accounts of the same subject and determine which details are emphasized in each medium. (R)
I can evaluate the advantages and disadvantages of presenting a subject in different mediums. (R)

Vocabulary

Informational Text

CCR

Delineate and evaluate the argument and specific claims in a text, including the validity of the reasoning as well as the relevance and sufficiency of the evidence.

Standard

Delineate and evaluate the argument and specific claims in a text, assessing whether the reasoning is valid and the evidence is relevant and sufficient; identify false statements and fallacious reasoning.

Enduring Understanding

To gain keener insight into the integration of knowledge and ideas, effective readers analyze and evaluate content, reasoning, and claims in diverse formats.

Essential Questions

In what ways does creative choice impact an audience?
Whose story is it, and why does it matter?

Suggested Learning Targets

I can identify the side of an argument an author presents in a text. (K)
I can determine the credibility of the author and his/her purpose (who wrote it, when it was written, and why it was written). (R)
I can identify claims that are supported by fact(s) and those that are opinion(s). (K)
I can recognize when an author introduces irrelevant evidence (unrelated or unnecessary evidence), false statements, and/or fallacious reasoning (incorrect reasoning – *People who sneeze have allergies, Katy sneezed, so she must be allergic to something.*) to his/her argument. (R)
I can delineate and evaluate an argument using the evidence an author provides and determine if the evidence provided is relevant and sufficient enough to support the claim. (R)

Vocabulary

delineate, argument, credibility, claim, relevant, sufficient, fallacious reasoning

Informational Text

CCR

Analyze how two or more texts address similar themes or topics in order to build knowledge or to compare the approaches the authors take.

Standard

Analyze seminal U.S. documents of historical and literary significance (e.g., Washington's Farewell Address, the Gettysburg Address, Roosevelt's Four Freedoms speech, King's "Letter from Birmingham Jail"), including how they address related themes and concepts.

Enduring Understanding

To gain keener insight into the integration of knowledge and ideas, effective readers analyze and evaluate content, reasoning, and claims in diverse formats.

Essential Questions

In what ways does creative choice impact an audience?
Whose story is it, and why does it matter?

Suggested Learning Targets

I can identify seminal U.S. documents that have related themes and concepts. (K)
I can analyze how different documents address related themes and concepts. (R)
I can determine how the time period and point of view of an author affects his/her perspective on a theme or concept. (R)

Vocabulary

seminal documents

R   RI.9-10.9

Informational Text

CCR

Read and comprehend complex literary and informational texts independently and proficiently.

Standard

By the end of grade 9, read and comprehend literary nonfiction in the grades 9–10 text complexity band proficiently, with scaffolding as needed at the high end of the range.

Enduring Understanding

Students who are college and career ready read and interpret a variety of complex texts with confidence and independence.

Essential Questions

What do good readers do?
Am I clear about what I just read?
How do I know?

Suggested Learning Targets

I can closely read complex grade level texts. (S)
I can reread a text to find more information or clarify ideas. (S)
I can use reading strategies (e.g., ask questions, make connections, take notes, make inferences, visualize, re-read) to help me understand difficult complex text. (S)

Vocabulary

(No applicable vocabulary)

R   RI.9.10

Informational Text

CCR

Read and comprehend complex literary and informational texts independently and proficiently.

Standard

By the end of grade 10, read and comprehend literary nonfiction at the high end of the grades 9–10 text complexity band independently and proficiently.

Enduring Understanding

Students who are college and career ready read and interpret a variety of complex texts with confidence and independence.

Essential Questions

What do good readers do?
Am I clear about what I just read?
How do I know?

Suggested Learning Targets

I can closely read complex grade level texts. (S)
I can reread a text to find more information or clarify ideas. (S)
I can use reading strategies (e.g., ask questions, make connections, take notes, make inferences, visualize, re-read) to help me understand difficult complex text. (S)

Vocabulary

(No applicable vocabulary)

R

RI.10.10

Writing

CCR

Write arguments to support claims in an analysis of substantive topics or texts, using valid reasoning and relevant and sufficient evidence.

Standard

Write arguments to support claims in an analysis of substantive topics or texts, using valid reasoning and relevant and sufficient evidence.

a. Introduce precise claim(s), distinguish the claim(s) from alternate or opposing claims, and create an organization that establishes clear relationships among claim(s), counterclaims, reasons, and evidence.

b. Develop claim(s) and counterclaims fairly, supplying evidence for each while pointing out the strengths and limitations of both in a manner that anticipates the audience's knowledge level and concerns.

c. Use words, phrases, and clauses to link the major sections of the text, create cohesion, and clarify the relationships between claim(s) and reasons, between reasons and evidence, and between claim(s) and counterclaims.

d. Establish and maintain a formal style and objective tone while attending to the norms and conventions of the discipline in which they are writing.

e. Provide a concluding statement or section that follows from and supports the argument presented.

*These broad types of writing include many subgenres. See Appendix A for definitions of key writing types.

Enduring Understanding

Writing should be purposely focused, detailed, organized, and sequenced in a way that clearly communicates the ideas to the reader.

Essential Questions

What do good writers do?
What's my purpose and how do I develop it?

Suggested Learning Targets

I can analyze substantive (influential) topics or texts to determine an argument that causes or has caused a debate in society. (K)

(continued on next page)

Vocabulary

debate, argument, claim, counterclaim, evidence, credible sources, transition

W

W.9-10.1

Writing

CCR

Write arguments to support claims in an analysis of substantive topics or texts, using valid reasoning and relevant and sufficient evidence.

Standard

Write arguments to support claims in an analysis of substantive topics or texts, using valid reasoning and relevant and sufficient evidence.

a. Introduce precise claim(s), distinguish the claim(s) from alternate or opposing claims, and create an organization that establishes clear relationships among claim(s), counterclaims, reasons, and evidence.

b. Develop claim(s) and counterclaims fairly, supplying evidence for each while pointing out the strengths and limitations of both in a manner that anticipates the audience's knowledge level and concerns.

c. Use words, phrases, and clauses to link the major sections of the text, create cohesion, and clarify the relationships between claim(s) and reasons, between reasons and evidence, and between claim(s) and counterclaims.

d. Establish and maintain a formal style and objective tone while attending to the norms and conventions of the discipline in which they are writing.

e. Provide a concluding statement or section that follows from and supports the argument presented.

*These broad types of writing include many subgenres. See Appendix A for definitions of key writing types.

Suggested Learning Targets

(continued from previous page)

I can choose a side of the argument and identify claims that support my choice and claims that oppose my choice. (R)

I can determine the credibility of a source (who wrote it, when it was written, and why it was written) and the accuracy of the details presented in the source. (R)

I can support my claims and counterclaims by pointing out the strengths and limitations of both with textual evidence ("word for word" support) found in credible sources. (R)

I can present my argument in a formal style that includes an introduction, supporting details with transitions that create cohesion and clarify relationships, and provide a concluding statement/section that supports my argument. (P)

Writing

CCR

Write informative/explanatory texts to examine and convey complex ideas and information clearly and accurately through the effective selection, organization, and analysis of content.

Standard

Write informative/explanatory texts to examine and convey complex ideas, concepts, and information clearly and accurately through the effective selection, organization, and analysis of content.

a. Introduce a topic; organize complex ideas, concepts, and information to make important connections and distinctions; include formatting (e.g., headings), graphics (e.g., figures, tables), and multimedia when useful to aiding comprehension.

b. Develop the topic with well-chosen, relevant, and sufficient facts, extended definitions, concrete details, quotations, or other information and examples appropriate to the audience's knowledge of the topic.

c. Use appropriate and varied transitions to link the major sections of the text, create cohesion, and clarify the relationships among complex ideas and concepts.

d. Use precise language and domain-specific vocabulary to manage the complexity of the topic.

e. Establish and maintain a formal style and objective tone while attending to the norms and conventions of the discipline in which they are writing.

f. Provide a concluding statement or section that follows from and supports the information or explanation presented (e.g., articulating implications or the significance of the topic).

These broad types of writing include many subgenres. See Appendix A for definitions of key writing types.

Enduring Understanding

Writing should be purposely focused, detailed, organized, and sequenced in a way that clearly communicates the ideas to the reader.

Essential Questions

What do good writers do?
What's my purpose and how do I develop it?

Suggested Learning Targets

I can select a topic and identify and gather relevant information (e.g., well-chosen facts, extended definitions, concrete details, quotations, examples) to share with my audience. (R)

(continued on next page)

Vocabulary

organizational structure, formatting structure, domain-specific vocabulary, transition, cohesion

W   **W.9-10.2**

Writing

CCR

Write informative/explanatory texts to examine and convey complex ideas and information clearly and accurately through the effective selection, organization, and analysis of content.

Standard

Write informative/explanatory texts to examine and convey complex ideas, concepts, and information clearly and accurately through the effective selection, organization, and analysis of content.

 a. Introduce a topic; organize complex ideas, concepts, and information to make important connections and distinctions; include formatting (e.g., headings), graphics (e.g., figures, tables), and multimedia when useful to aiding comprehension.
 b. Develop the topic with well-chosen, relevant, and sufficient facts, extended definitions, concrete details, quotations, or other information and examples appropriate to the audience's knowledge of the topic.
 c. Use appropriate and varied transitions to link the major sections of the text, create cohesion, and clarify the relationships among complex ideas and concepts.
 d. Use precise language and domain-specific vocabulary to manage the complexity of the topic.
 e. Establish and maintain a formal style and objective tone while attending to the norms and conventions of the discipline in which they are writing.
 f. Provide a concluding statement or section that follows from and supports the information or explanation presented (e.g., articulating implications or the significance of the topic).

These broad types of writing include many subgenres. See Appendix A for definitions of key writing types.

Suggested Learning Targets

(continued from previous page)

I can define common organizational/formatting structures (e.g., headings, graphics, multimedia) and determine the structure(s) that will allow me to organize my complex ideas best. (R)

I can analyze the information, identify domain-specific vocabulary for my topic, and organize information into broader categories using my chosen structure(s). (R)

I can present my information maintaining an objective tone and formal style that includes an introduction that previews what is to follow, supporting details, varied transitions (to clarify and create cohesion when I move from one idea to another), and a concluding statement/section that supports the information presented. (P)

Writing

CCR

Write narratives to develop real or imagined experiences or events using effective technique, well-chosen details, and well-structured event sequences.

Standard

Write narratives to develop real or imagined experiences or events using effective technique, well-chosen details, and well-structured event sequences.

a. Engage and orient the reader by setting out a problem, situation, or observation, establishing one or multiple point(s) of view, and introducing a narrator and/or characters; create a smooth progression of experiences or events.

b. Use narrative techniques, such as dialogue, pacing, description, reflection, and multiple plot lines, to develop experiences, events, and/or characters.

c. Use a variety of techniques to sequence events so that they build on one another to create a coherent whole.

d. Use precise words and phrases, telling details, and sensory language to convey a vivid picture of the experiences, events, setting, and/or characters.

e. Provide a conclusion that follows from and reflects on what is experienced, observed, or resolved over the course of the narrative.

*These broad types of writing include many subgenres. See Appendix A for definitions of key writing types.

Enduring Understanding

Writing should be purposely focused, detailed, organized, and sequenced in a way that clearly communicates the ideas to the reader.

Essential Questions

What do good writers do?
What's my purpose and how do I develop it?

Suggested Learning Targets

I can define narrative and describe the basic parts of plot (exposition, rising action, climax, falling action, and resolution). (K)

(continued on next page)

Vocabulary

narrative, point of view, plot line, transition

W

W.9-10.3

Writing

CCR

Write narratives to develop real or imagined experiences or events using effective technique, well-chosen details, and well-structured event sequences.

Standard

Write narratives to develop real or imagined experiences or events using effective technique, well-chosen details, and well-structured event sequences.

a. Engage and orient the reader by setting out a problem, situation, or observation, establishing one or multiple point(s) of view, and introducing a narrator and/or characters; create a smooth progression of experiences or events.

b. Use narrative techniques, such as dialogue, pacing, description, reflection, and multiple plot lines, to develop experiences, events, and/or characters.

c. Use a variety of techniques to sequence events so that they build on one another to create a coherent whole.

d. Use precise words and phrases, telling details, and sensory language to convey a vivid picture of the experiences, events, setting, and/or characters.

e. Provide a conclusion that follows from and reflects on what is experienced, observed, or resolved over the course of the narrative.

*These broad types of writing include many subgenres. See Appendix A for definitions of key writing types.

Suggested Learning Targets

(continued from previous page)

I can engage the reader by introducing one or more point(s) of view, the narrator (first, second, or third person point of view), characters, setting (set the scene), and the event that starts the story in motion. (S)

I can use narrative techniques (e.g., dialogue, pacing, description, reflection, and/or multiple plot lines) to develop experiences, events, and/or characters where one event logically leads to another. (S)

I can use descriptive words and phrases that reveal details, appeal to the senses, and help convey a vivid picture of the experiences, events, setting, and/or characters (create mind pictures). (S)

I can signal changes in time and place by using transition words, phrases, and clauses to show the relationships among experiences and events. (S)

I can write a logical conclusion that reflects on the experiences/events and provides a sense of closure (ties up all loose ends and leaves the reader satisfied). (P)

Writing

CCR

Produce clear and coherent writing in which the development, organization, and style are appropriate to task, purpose, and audience.

Standard

Produce clear and coherent writing in which the development, organization, and style are appropriate to task, purpose, and audience. (Grade-specific expectations for writing types are defined in standards 1–3 above.)

Enduring Understanding

Producing clear ideas as a writer involves selecting appropriate style and structure for an audience and is strengthened through revision and technology.

Essential Questions

Writing clearly: What makes a difference?

Suggested Learning Targets

I can identify the writing style (argument, informative/explanatory, or narrative) that best fits my task, purpose, and audience. (K)

I can use organizational/formatting structures (graphic organizers) to develop my writing ideas. (S)

I can compose a clear and logical piece of writing that demonstrates my understanding of a specific writing style. (P)

Vocabulary

writing style, task, purpose, audience

W

W.9-10.4

Writing

CCR

Develop and strengthen writing as needed by planning, revising, editing, rewriting, or trying a new approach.

Standard

Develop and strengthen writing as needed by planning, revising, editing, rewriting, or trying a new approach, focusing on addressing what is most significant for a specific purpose and audience. (Editing for conventions should demonstrate command of Language standards 1–3 up to and including grades 9–10.)

Enduring Understanding

Producing clear ideas as a writer involves selecting appropriate style and structure for an audience and is strengthened through revision and technology.

Essential Questions

Writing clearly: What makes a difference?

Suggested Learning Targets

- I can use prewriting strategies to formulate ideas (e.g., graphic organizers, brainstorming, lists). (S)
- I can recognize that a well-developed piece of writing requires more than one draft. (K)
- I can apply revision strategies (e.g., reading aloud, checking for misunderstandings, adding and deleting details) with the help of others. (S)
- I can edit my writing by checking for errors in capitalization, punctuation, grammar, spelling, etc. (S)
- I can analyze my writing to determine if my purpose and audience have been fully addressed and revise when necessary. (S)
- I can prepare multiple drafts using revisions and edits to develop and strengthen my writing. (P)
- I can recognize when revising, editing, and rewriting are not enough, and I need to try a new approach. (R)

Vocabulary

revision strategy, edit, purpose, audience

Writing

CCR

Use technology, including the Internet, to produce and publish writing and to interact and collaborate with others.

Standard

Use technology, including the Internet, to produce, publish, and update individual or shared writing products, taking advantage of technology's capacity to link to other information and to display information flexibly and dynamically.

Enduring Understanding

Producing clear ideas as a writer involves selecting appropriate style and structure for an audience and is strengthened through revision and technology.

Essential Questions

Writing clearly: What makes a difference?

Suggested Learning Targets

I can identify technology (e.g., Word, Publisher, PowerPoint, wiki, blog) that will help me produce, publish, and update my individual or shared writing products. (K)

I can determine the most efficient technology medium to complete my writing task. (S)

I can use technology to enhance my writing product by linking to other information and/or displaying information flexibly and dynamically. (S)

Vocabulary

flexibly, dynamically

W

W.9-10.6

Writing

CCR

Conduct short as well as more sustained research projects based on focused questions, demonstrating understanding of the subject under investigation.

Standard

Conduct short as well as more sustained research projects to answer a question (including a self-generated question) or solve a problem; narrow or broaden the inquiry when appropriate; synthesize multiple sources on the subject, demonstrating understanding of the subject under investigation.

Enduring Understanding	Essential Questions
Effective research presents an answer to a question, demonstrates understanding of the inquiry, and properly cites information from multiple sources.	What do good researchers do? "Cut and Paste:" What's the problem?

Suggested Learning Targets

I can define research and distinguish how research differs from other types of writing. (K)

I can focus my research around a problem to be solved, a central question that is provided, or a self-generated question I have determined (e.g., *How did Edgar Allan Poe's life experiences influence his writing style?*). (S)

I can choose several sources (e.g., biographies, non-fiction texts, online encyclopedia) and synthesize information to answer my research inquiry. (R)

I can determine if I need to narrow or broaden my inquiry based on the information gathered. (R)

I can demonstrate understanding of the subject under investigation. (P)

Vocabulary

research, central question, synthesize

W.

W . 9-10.7

Writing

CCR

Gather relevant information from multiple print and digital sources, assess the credibility and accuracy of each source, and integrate the information while avoiding plagiarism.

Standard

Gather relevant information from multiple authoritative print and digital sources, using advanced searches effectively; assess the usefulness of each source in answering the research question; integrate information into the text selectively to maintain the flow of ideas, avoiding plagiarism and following a standard format for citation.

Enduring Understanding

Effective research presents an answer to a question, demonstrates understanding of the inquiry, and properly cites information from multiple sources.

Essential Questions

What do good researchers do?
"Cut and Paste:" What's the problem?

Suggested Learning Targets

I can determine the credibility of a source by reviewing who wrote it, when it was written, and why it was written. (R)

I can assess the usefulness of my sources to determine those that contain the information that best answers my research question. (S)

I can use advanced searches with multiple authoritative print and/or digital sources effectively to gather information needed to support my research. (S)

I can define plagiarism (using someone else's words/ideas as my own). (K)

I can avoid plagiarism by paraphrasing (putting in my own words) and/or summarizing my research findings. (S)

I can determine when my research data or facts must be quoted (directly stated "word for word") and integrate the information into my text to maintain the flow of ideas. (S)

I can follow a standard format for citation to create a bibliography for sources that I paraphrased or quoted in my writing. (K)

Vocabulary

credibility, advanced search, plagiarism, paraphrase, authoritative print

W   **W.9-10.8**

Writing

CCR

Draw evidence from literary or informational texts to support analysis, reflection, and research.

Standard

Draw evidence from literary or informational texts to support analysis, reflection, and research.

a. Apply *grades 9–10 Reading standards* to literature (e.g., "Analyze how an author draws on and transforms source material in a specific work [e.g., how Shakespeare treats a theme or topic from Ovid or the Bible or how a later author draws on a play by Shakespeare]").

b. Apply *grades 9–10 Reading standards* to literary nonfiction (e.g., "Delineate and evaluate the argument and specific claims in a text, assessing whether the reasoning is valid and the evidence is relevant and sufficient; identify false statements and fallacious reasoning").

Enduring Understanding

Effective research presents an answer to a question, demonstrates understanding of the inquiry, and properly cites information from multiple sources.

Essential Questions

What do good researchers do?
"Cut and Paste:" What's the problem?

Suggested Learning Targets

I can define textual evidence ("word for word" support). (K)
I can determine textual evidence that supports my analysis, reflection, and/or research. (R)
I can compose written responses and include textual evidence to strengthen my analysis, reflection, and/or research. (P)

Vocabulary

textual evidence, analysis, reflection, research

W -

Writing

CCR

Write routinely over extended time frames (time for research, reflection, and revision) and shorter time frames (a single sitting or a day or two) for a range of tasks, purposes, and audiences.

Standard

Write routinely over extended time frames (time for research, reflection, and revision) and shorter time frames (a single sitting or a day or two) for a range of tasks, purposes, and audiences.

Enduring Understanding

Effective writers use a variety of formats to communicate ideas appropriate for the audience, task, and time frame.

Essential Questions

Why write?
What do good writers do?

Suggested Learning Targets

I can recognize that different writing tasks (e.g., journal, reflection, research) require varied time frames to complete. (K)
I can determine a writing format/style to fit my task, purpose, and/or audience. (R)
I can write for a variety of reasons (e.g., to inform, to describe, to persuade, to entertain/convey an experience). (P)

Vocabulary

writing format, writing style, task, purpose, audience

W

W.9-10.10

Speaking and Listening

CCR

Prepare for and participate effectively in a range of conversations and collaborations with diverse partners, building on others' ideas and expressing their own clearly and persuasively.

Standard

Initiate and participate effectively in a range of collaborative discussions (one-on-one, in groups, and teacher-led) with diverse partners on *grades 9–10 topics, texts, and issues,* building on others' ideas and expressing their own clearly and persuasively.

a. Come to discussions prepared, having read and researched material under study; explicitly draw on that preparation by referring to evidence from texts and other research on the topic or issue to stimulate a thoughtful, well-reasoned exchange of ideas.

b. Work with peers to set rules for collegial discussions and decision-making (e.g., informal consensus, taking votes on key issues, presentation of alternate views), clear goals and deadlines, and individual roles as needed.

c. Propel conversations by posing and responding to questions that relate the current discussion to broader themes or larger ideas; actively incorporate others into the discussion; and clarify, verify, or challenge ideas and conclusions.

d. Respond thoughtfully to diverse perspectives, summarize points of agreement and disagreement, and, when warranted, qualify or justify their own views and understanding and make new connections in light of the evidence and reasoning presented.

Enduring Understanding

Comprehension is enhanced through a collaborative process of sharing and evaluating ideas.

Essential Questions

What makes collaboration meaningful?
Making meaning from a variety of sources: What will help?

Suggested Learning Targets

I can review and/or research material(s) to be discussed and determine key points and/or central ideas. (R)

(continued on next page)

Vocabulary

elaborate, integrate, warranted, justify

SL

SL.9-10.1

Speaking and Listening

CCR

Prepare for and participate effectively in a range of conversations and collaborations with diverse partners, building on others' ideas and expressing their own clearly and persuasively.

Standard

Initiate and participate effectively in a range of collaborative discussions (one-on-one, in groups, and teacher-led) with diverse partners on *grades 9–10 topics, texts, and issues,* building on others' ideas and expressing their own clearly and persuasively.

a. Come to discussions prepared, having read and researched material under study; explicitly draw on that preparation by referring to evidence from texts and other research on the topic or issue to stimulate a thoughtful, well-reasoned exchange of ideas.

b. Work with peers to set rules for collegial discussions and decision-making (e.g., informal consensus, taking votes on key issues, presentation of alternate views), clear goals and deadlines, and individual roles as needed.

c. Propel conversations by posing and responding to questions that relate the current discussion to broader themes or larger ideas; actively incorporate others into the discussion; and clarify, verify, or challenge ideas and conclusions.

d. Respond thoughtfully to diverse perspectives, summarize points of agreement and disagreement, and, when warranted, qualify or justify their own views and understanding and make new connections in light of the evidence and reasoning presented.

Suggested Learning Targets

(continued from previous page)

I can create questions and locate key textual evidence to contribute to a discussion on the given topic, text, or issue. (P)

I can work with peers to define the rules and roles necessary for collegial discussions and decision-making. (S)

I can come prepared with key points and textual evidence to contribute to a discussion and stimulate a thoughtful well-reasoned exchange of ideas. (S)

I can participate in a discussion by posing questions that connect the ideas of several speakers, responding to questions, and elaborating on my own ideas and/or the ideas of others to propel the discussion. (S)

I can make relevant observations and use my ideas and comments to relate the current discussion to broader themes or ideas. (S)

I can respond thoughtfully to diverse perspectives presented in a discussion, integrate them with my own when warranted (appropriate), and justify my own views based on evidence introduced by others. (S)

Speaking and Listening

CCR

Integrate and evaluate information presented in diverse media and formats, including visually, quantitatively, and orally.

Standard

Integrate multiple sources of information presented in diverse media or formats (e.g., visually, quantitatively, orally) evaluating the credibility and accuracy of each source.

Enduring Understanding

Comprehension is enhanced through a collaborative process of sharing and evaluating ideas.

Essential Questions

What makes collaboration meaningful? Making meaning from a variety of sources: What will help?

Suggested Learning Targets

I can identify various purposes (e.g., to inform, to persuade, to describe, to convey an experience) for presenting information to a reader or audience. (K)
I can analyze the information presented in diverse media and formats (e.g., charts, graphs, tables, websites, speeches) and integrate the information to gain an overall understanding of the topic presented. (R)
I can evaluate the credibility and accuracy of various presentations. (R)

Vocabulary

media, format

SL   SL.9-10.2

Speaking and Listening

CCR

Evaluate a speaker's point of view, reasoning, and use of evidence and rhetoric.

Standard

Evaluate a speaker's point of view, reasoning, and use of evidence and rhetoric, identifying any fallacious reasoning or exaggerated or distorted evidence.

Enduring Understanding	Essential Questions
Comprehension is enhanced through a collaborative process of sharing and evaluating ideas.	What makes collaboration meaningful? Making meaning from a variety of sources: What will help?

Suggested Learning Targets

I can define point of view as how the speaker feels about the situation/topic being presented. (K)

I can determine a speaker's point of view (*What do I know about the speaker's opinions, values, and/or beliefs?*) and explain his/her reasoning. (R)

I can define rhetoric (a technique used to persuade a listener to consider a topic from a different perspective). (K)

I can identify when a speaker uses evidence and/or rhetoric and analyze how these techniques strengthen his/her point of view or purpose. (R)

I can recognize when a speaker introduces distorted evidence (unjust interpretation) and/or fallacious reasoning (incorrect reasoning – *People who sneeze have allergies. Katy sneezed, so she must be allergic to something.*) to his/her argument. (K)

Vocabulary

point of view, rhetoric, distorted evidence, fallacious reasoning

SL

SL.9-10.3

Speaking and Listening

CCR

Present information, findings, and supporting evidence such that listeners can follow the line of reasoning and the organization, development, and style are appropriate to task, purpose, and audience.

Standard

Present information, findings, and supporting evidence clearly, concisely, and logically such that listeners can follow the line of reasoning and the organization, development, substance, and style are appropriate to purpose, audience, and task.

Enduring Understanding

Presentation of knowledge and ideas is enhanced through appropriate organization and style for an audience via the use of visual displays, technology, and the appropriate use of language.

Essential Questions

What makes a presentation "great"?
"What I say" versus "how I say it", does it really matter?

Suggested Learning Targets

I can present information, findings, and/or supporting evidence clearly, concisely, and logically. (P)

I can present my information in a sequence that allows the listener to follow my line of reasoning. (P)

I can prepare a presentation with organization, development, substance, and style that are appropriate to purpose, task, and audience. (P)

Vocabulary

line of reasoning, task, purpose, audience

Speaking and Listening

CCR

Make strategic use of digital media and visual displays of data to express information and enhance understanding of presentations.

Standard

Make strategic use of digital media (e.g., textual, graphical, audio, visual, and interactive elements) in presentations to enhance understanding of findings, reasoning, and evidence and to add interest.

Enduring Understanding

Presentation of knowledge and ideas is enhanced through appropriate organization and style for an audience via the use of visual displays, technology, and the appropriate use of language.

Essential Questions

What makes a presentation "great"?
"What I say" versus "how I say it", does it really matter?

Suggested Learning Targets

I can identify the parts of my presentation, including findings, reasoning, and evidence, that could use clarification, strengthening, and/or additional interest. (K)
I can integrate appropriate digital media in a strategic manner to improve my presentation. (S)

Vocabulary

digital media

SL

SL.9-10.5

Speaking and Listening

CCR

Adapt speech to a variety of contexts and communicative tasks, demonstrating command of formal English when indicated or appropriate.

Standard

Adapt speech to a variety of contexts and tasks, demonstrating command of formal English when indicated or appropriate. (See grades 9–10 Language standards 1 and 3 for specific expectations.)

Enduring Understanding

Presentation of knowledge and ideas is enhanced through appropriate organization and style for an audience via the use of visual displays, technology, and the appropriate use of language.

Essential Questions

What makes a presentation "great"?
"What I say" versus "how I say it", does it really matter?

Suggested Learning Targets

I can identify various reasons for speaking (e.g., informational, descriptive, formal, informal). (K)
I can determine speaking tasks that will require a formal structure. (R)
I can compose a formal speech that demonstrates a command of grades 9-10 Language standards. (P)

Vocabulary

formal, informal

Language

CCR

Demonstrate command of the conventions of standard English grammar and usage when writing or speaking.

Standard

Demonstrate command of the conventions of standard English grammar and usage when writing or speaking.

a. Use parallel structure.*
b. Use various types of phrases (noun, verb, adjectival, adverbial, participial, prepositional, absolute) and clauses (independent, dependent; noun, relative, adverbial) to convey specific meanings and add variety and interest to writing or presentations.

* See ELA CCSS Appendix A, page 31 for Language Progressive Skills.

Enduring Understanding

Effective communication of ideas when speaking or writing relies on the appropriate use of the conventions of language.

Essential Questions

Why do the rules of language matter? Communicating clearly: What does it take?

Suggested Learning Targets

I can define and identify parallel structures (using similar patterns of words, phrases, or clauses to show the same level of importance). (K)

I can recognize when I have not used parallel structure in my writing (e.g., *I would like to go skiing, hiking, and on a bike ride. SHOULD BE I would like to go skiing, hiking, and biking.*). (K)

I can use parallel structure correctly in my writing. (S)

I can define and identify various types of phrases and clauses. (K)

I can use appropriate phrases and clauses to convey specific meaning and add variety and interest to writing or presentations. (S)

Vocabulary

parallel structure, phrases, clauses

L

L.9-10.1

Language

CCR

Demonstrate command of the conventions of standard English capitalization, punctuation, and spelling when writing.

Standard

Demonstrate command of the conventions of standard English capitalization, punctuation, and spelling when writing.

a. Use a semicolon (and perhaps a conjunctive adverb) to link two or more closely related independent clauses.
b. Use a colon to introduce a list or quotation.
c. Spell correctly.

Enduring Understanding	Essential Questions
Effective communication of ideas when speaking or writing relies on the appropriate use of the conventions of language.	Why do the rules of language matter? Communicating clearly: What does it take?

Suggested Learning Targets

I can determine when to capitalize words (e.g., proper nouns, "I", first word in a sentence). (K)

I can identify and explain when to use semicolons (to connect closely related independent clauses with or without conjunctive adverbs). (R)

I can use a semicolon with a conjunctive adverb (e.g., *Sydney is a brilliant writer; therefore, she wins writing contests all the time.*). (S)

I can identify and explain when to use a colon (to introduce a list or quotation). (R)

I can use a colon to introduce a list (e.g., *London has all of her supplies for school: pencils, paper, highlighters, and a flashdrive.*) or quotation (e.g., *Anna's favorite quote is by Robert Frost: "A poem begins in delight and ends in wisdom."*). (S)

I can identify misspelled words and use resources to assist me in spelling correctly. (K)

Vocabulary

semicolon, independent clause, colon

L
L.9-10.2

Language

CCR

Apply knowledge of language to understand how language functions in different contexts, to make effective choices for meaning or style, and to comprehend more fully when reading or listening.

Standard

Apply knowledge of language to understand how language functions in different contexts, to make effective choices for meaning or style, and to comprehend more fully when reading or listening.

a. Write and edit work so that it conforms to the guidelines in a style manual (e.g., *MLA Handbook*, Turabian's *Manual for Writers*) appropriate for the discipline and writing type.

Enduring Understanding

Effective readers, writers, and listeners use knowledge of language to make appropriate choices when presenting information and to clarify meaning when reading or listening.

Essential Questions

How does situation affect meaning?
How does author's choice impact an audience?

Suggested Learning Targets

I can identify how language functions in different contexts. (K)
I can analyze the context of various texts and determine how language choice affects meaning, style, and comprehension. (R)
I can apply the guidelines in a given style manual to write and edit work. (S)

Vocabulary

context, style manual

L

L.9-10.3

Language

CCR

Determine or clarify the meaning of unknown and multiple-meaning words and phrases by using context clues, analyzing meaningful word parts, and consulting general and specialized reference materials, as appropriate.

Standard

Determine or clarify the meaning of unknown and multiple-meaning words and phrases based on *grades 9–10 reading and content*, choosing flexibly from a range of strategies.

a. Use context (e.g., the overall meaning of a sentence, paragraph, or text; a word's position or function in a sentence) as a clue to the meaning of a word or phrase.

b. Identify and correctly use patterns of word changes that indicate different meanings or parts of speech (e.g., *analyze, analysis, analytical; advocate, advocacy*).

c. Consult general and specialized reference materials (e.g., dictionaries, glossaries, thesauruses), both print and digital, to find the pronunciation of a word or determine or clarify its precise meaning, its part of speech, or its etymology.

d. Verify the preliminary determination of the meaning of a word or phrase (e.g., by checking the inferred meaning in context or in a dictionary).

Enduring Understanding	Essential Questions
Effective readers and writers use knowledge of the structure and context of language to acquire, clarify, and appropriately use vocabulary.	When a word doesn't make sense, what can I do? How do I use what I know to figure out what I don't know?

Suggested Learning Targets

I can infer the meaning of unknown words using context clues (e.g., definitions, synonyms/antonyms, restatements, examples found in surrounding text). (R)

I can recognize and define common affixes and roots (units of meaning). (K)

I can break down unknown words into units of meaning to infer the definition of the unknown word. (R)

I can use patterns of word changes to determine a word's meaning or part of speech. (S)

I can verify my inferred meaning of an unknown word, its part of speech, and/or its etymology by consulting general and specialized reference materials (e.g., dictionaries, glossaries, thesauruses). (K)

Vocabulary

affix, root, etymology

L   L.9-10.4

Language

CCR

Demonstrate understanding of word relationships and nuances in word meanings.

Standard

Demonstrate understanding of figurative language, word relationships, and nuances in word meanings.

a. Interpret figures of speech (e.g., euphemism, oxymoron) in context and analyze their role in the text.
b. Analyze nuances in the meaning of words with similar denotations.

Enduring Understanding

Effective readers and writers use knowledge of the structure and context of language to acquire, clarify, and appropriately use vocabulary.

Essential Questions

When a word doesn't make sense, what can I do?

How do I use what I know to figure out what I don't know?

Suggested Learning Targets

I can define and identify various forms of figurative language (e.g., simile, metaphor, hyperbole, personification, alliteration, onomatopoeia). (K)

I can interpret figures of speech (sometimes what you say is not exactly what you mean) and analyze their overall role in the text. (R)

I can recognize word relationships and use the relationships to further understand multiple words (e.g., *sympathetic/apathetic*). (S)

I can recognize the difference between denotative meanings (all words have a dictionary definition) and connotative meanings (some words carry feeling). (K)

I can analyze how certain words and phrases that have similar denotations (definitions) can carry different nuances (subtle shades of meaning, feeling, or tone). (R)

Vocabulary

figure of speech, word relationships, denotation, nuance

L
L.9-10.5

Language

CCR

Acquire and use accurately a range of general academic and domain-specific words and phrases sufficient for reading, writing, speaking, and listening at the college and career readiness level; demonstrate independence in gathering vocabulary knowledge when encountering an unknown term important to comprehension or expression.

Standard

Acquire and use accurately general academic and domain-specific words and phrases, sufficient for reading, writing, speaking, and listening at the college and career readiness level; demonstrate independence in gathering vocabulary knowledge when considering a word or phrase important to comprehension or expression.

Enduring Understanding	Essential Questions
Effective readers and writers use knowledge of the structure and context of language to acquire, clarify, and appropriately use vocabulary.	When a word doesn't make sense, what can I do? How do I use what I know to figure out what I don't know?

Suggested Learning Targets

I can recognize the difference between general academic words and phrases (Tier Two words are subtle or precise ways to say relatively simple things, e.g., *saunter* instead of *walk*.) and domain-specific words and phrases (Tier Three words are specific to content knowledge, e.g., *lava, legislature, carburetor*.).* (K)

I can acquire and use college and career readiness level academic and domain-specific words/phrases to demonstrate proficiency in reading, writing, speaking, and listening. (S)

I can consider vocabulary knowledge including denotation, nuance, etymology, etc. and determine the most appropriate words or phrases to express overall meaning. (S)

I can gather vocabulary knowledge independently when considering a word or phrase important to comprehension or expression. (S)

*Tier One, Tier Two, and Tier Three words are clarified on pages 33-35 of Appendix A in the Common Core Standards.

Vocabulary

general academic words, domain-specific words

L   L.9-10.6